AF279306

CARPE THAT F*CKING DIEM

summersdale

TO:
FROM:

WHEN'S THE BEST TIME TO START? NOW!

The envious moment is flying now, now, while we're speaking: seize the day.

HORACE

GET READY TO KICK SOME ASS TODAY!

WITH THE NEW
DAY COMES NEW
STRENGTH AND
NEW THOUGHTS.

Eleanor Roosevelt

OPPORTUNITIES MULTIPLY AS THEY ARE SEIZED.

SUN TZU

OPEN THE CURTAINS AND LET A NEW F*CKING DAY BEGIN!

Act as if what
you do makes a
difference. It does.

William James

You are never too old
to set another goal or to
dream a new dream.

LES BROWN

GET THE F*CK ON WITH IT!

IF YOU'RE GOING THROUGH HELL, KEEP GOING.

Anonymous

I'd rather regret the things
I've done than regret the
things I haven't done.

Lucille Ball

IT'S TIME TO STOP F*CKING AROUND!

If you obey all the rules,
you miss all the fun.

KATHARINE HEPBURN

WHEREVER YOU ARE — BE ALL THERE.

JIM ELLIOT

DIFFICULT DOESN'T MEAN IMPOSSIBLE.

EMBRACE THE F*CKING CHALLENGE!

ONE MAY WALK OVER THE HIGHEST MOUNTAIN ONE STEP AT A TIME.

John Wanamaker

Things do not happen.
Things are made to happen.

JOHN F. KENNEDY

GOOD THINGS COME TO THOSE WHO DON'T F*CKING WAIT

WHO SEEKS SHALL FIND.

Sophocles

IF YOU ASK ME
WHAT I CAME
INTO THIS LIFE
TO DO, I WILL
TELL YOU:
I CAME TO LIVE
OUT LOUD.

Émile Zola

TODAY IS A BLANK PAGE, SO FILL IT WITH BIG SHOUTY CAPITALS!

WHENEVER YOU FALL, PICK SOMETHING UP.

OSWALD AVERY

For myself, I am an optimist – it does not seem to be much use being anything else.

WINSTON CHURCHILL

GET OFF YOUR BACKSIDE!

Tell me, what is it you
plan to do with your one
wild and precious life?

Mary Oliver

EITHER YOU RUN THE DAY OR THE DAY RUNS YOU.

Jim Rohn

LIFE IS ABOUT TAKING PART – SEIZE THAT F*CKING DAY!

EXPECT PROBLEMS AND <u>EAT THEM FOR</u> <u>BREAKFAST.</u>

ALFRED A. MONTAPERT

I couldn't wait for success,
so I went ahead without it.

Jonathan Winters

GRAB LIFE BY THE BALLS!

Turn your face to the
sun and the shadows
fall behind you.

MAORI PROVERB

To know oneself,
one should
assert oneself.

ALBERT CAMUS

SHOOT
FOR THE
F*CKING
STARS!

I CAN,
THEREFORE
I AM.

Simone Weil

IN ORDER TO SUCCEED, WE MUST FIRST BELIEVE THAT WE CAN.

NIKOS KAZANTZAKIS

BE THE HERO OF YOUR OWN FREAKIN' STORY!

You must be the change you wish to see in the world.

Mahatma Gandhi

Life is simple –
it's just not easy.

ANONYMOUS

WHAT ARE YOU WAITING FOR? A F*CKING INVITATION?

ALL LIFE IS AN EXPERIMENT. THE MORE EXPERIMENTS YOU MAKE, THE BETTER.

Ralph Waldo Emerson

No one knows what
he can do till he tries.

Publilius Syrus

GET A

F*CKING

GRIP

Life is a shipwreck,
but we must not forget
to sing in the lifeboats.

VOLTAIRE

LIFE ISN'T ABOUT FINDING YOURSELF. LIFE IS ABOUT <u>CREATING</u> <u>YOURSELF</u>.

GEORGE BERNARD SHAW

MAKE A WISH... THEN MAKE IT F*CKING COME TRUE!

WHETHER YOU
THINK YOU CAN
OR YOU THINK
YOU CAN'T,
YOU'RE RIGHT.

Henry Ford

> Do what you can, with what you have, where you are.

THEODORE ROOSEVELT

YO-

F*CKING-

LO

WHEN YOU REACH THE END OF YOUR ROPE, TIE A KNOT IN IT AND HANG ON.

Anonymous

PERSEVERANCE
IS FAILING
NINETEEN TIMES
AND SUCCEEDING
THE TWENTIETH.

Julie Andrews

WHEN LIFE THROWS TOMATOES AT YOU, MAKE A BLOODY MARY!

SET YOUR GOALS HIGH, AND DON'T STOP TILL YOU GET THERE.

BO JACKSON

The man who removes a mountain begins by carrying away small stones.

CHINESE PROVERB

FOR F*CK'S SAKE, PUT YOURSELF OUT THERE!

Opportunity does not knock – it presents itself when you beat down the door.

Kyle Chandler

NOTHING IS A WASTE OF TIME IF YOU USE THE EXPERIENCE WISELY.

Auguste Rodin

YOU COULD RUN
IN THE RACE,
OR F*CKING
ORGANIZE IT

IT'S ALWAYS TOO EARLY TO QUIT.

NORMAN VINCENT PEALE

Find ecstasy in life;
the mere sense of
living is joy enough.

Emily Dickinson

QUIT PROCRASTINATING

If you wait, all that happens is that you get older.

MARIO ANDRETTI

One joy scatters
a hundred griefs.

CHINESE PROVERB

STILL ON THE SOFA? COME ON, DUDE!

LIFE IS EITHER
A DARING
ADVENTURE
OR NOTHING.

Helen Keller

YOU'RE THE BLACKSMITH OF YOUR OWN HAPPINESS.

SWEDISH PROVERB

SHOW THE WORLD WHAT YOU'RE F*CKING MADE OF!

How wonderful it is that nobody need wait a single moment before starting to improve the world.

Anne Frank

Opportunities are like sunrises. If you wait too long, you miss them.

WILLIAM ARTHUR WARD

MAKE IT
F*CKING
HAPPEN

THERE ARE
ALWAYS
FLOWERS
FOR THOSE
WHO WANT
TO SEE
THEM.

Henri Matisse

It's OK to have butterflies in your stomach. Just get them to fly in formation.

Rob Gilbert

TO REST IS TO RUST, SO BE A WELL-OILED MACHINE!

We are all in the gutter
but some of us are
looking at the stars.

OSCAR WILDE

SOME DAYS THERE WON'T BE A SONG IN YOUR HEART. <u>SING ANYWAY.</u>

EMORY AUSTIN

WORK YOUR FREAKIN' MAGIC!

NOTHING WILL
WORK UNLESS
YOU DO.

Maya Angelou

The secret of getting
ahead is getting started.

ANONYMOUS

GET YOUR ASS IN GEAR

THE WISE DOES AT ONCE WHAT THE FOOL DOES AT LAST.

Baltasar Gracián

SETTING GOALS
IS THE FIRST STEP
IN TURNING THE
INVISIBLE INTO
THE VISIBLE.

Tony Robbins

GET OUT THERE AND HAVE SOME F*CKING FUN!

YOU CAN'T TURN BACK THE CLOCK BUT YOU CAN WIND IT UP AGAIN.

BONNIE PRUDDEN

Live today, for tomorrow
it will all be history.

PROVERB

YOU'RE F*CKING AMAZING!

If you can find a path with
no obstacles, it probably
doesn't lead anywhere.

Frank A. Clark

BE HAPPY. IT'S ONE WAY OF BEING WISE.

Colette

CARPE
THAT DIEM SO
F*CKIN' HARD!

A JOURNEY OF A THOUSAND MILES BEGINS WITH A SINGLE STEP.

LAO TZU

The most important thing is to enjoy your life – to be happy. It's all that matters.

Audrey Hepburn

LIVE AND F*CKING LAUGH

The best way to predict the future is to create it.

ANONYMOUS

Every artist was
first an amateur.

RALPH WALDO EMERSON

PEDAL TO THE F*CKING METAL!

LIFE SHRINKS OR EXPANDS IN PROPORTION TO ONE'S COURAGE.

Anaïs Nin

THE BEST WAY TO MAKE YOUR DREAMS COME TRUE IS TO WAKE UP.

PAUL VALÉRY

IF AT FIRST
YOU DON'T
SUCCEED, TRY
A-F*CKING-GAIN

I have never met a man
so ignorant that I couldn't
learn something from him.

Galileo Galilei

To me, every hour of the day
and night is an unspeakably
perfect miracle.

WALT WHITMAN

F*CKING DO SOMETHING! ANYTHING!

LIFE IS A HELLUVA LOT MORE FUN IF YOU SAY 'YES' RATHER THAN 'NO'.

Richard Branson

To succeed in life,
you need three things:
a wishbone, a backbone
and a funny bone.

Reba McEntire

MAKE YOUR OWN F*CKING SUNSHINE!

Look at life through
the windshield,
not the rear-view mirror.

BYRD BAGGETT

THE BEST WAY OUT IS ALWAYS THROUGH.

ROBERT FROST

YOU CAN DO IT. ALL YOU HAVE TO DO IS F*CKING TRY!

LOOK AT
EVERYTHING AS
THOUGH YOU
WERE SEEING IT
FOR THE FIRST
OR LAST TIME.

Betty Smith

Nothing really matters
except what you do now
in this instant of time.

EILEEN CADDY

JUST BE YOURSELF: A F*CKING LEGEND

BEGIN TO BE NOW WHAT YOU WILL BE HEREAFTER.

William James

IF YOUR SHIP
DOESN'T COME IN,
SWIM OUT TO IT.

Jonathan Winters

BE WHO
YOU'VE ALWAYS
WANTED TO BE.
BE A F*CKING
ASTRONAUT,
IF YOU WANT!

ATTITUDE IS EVERYTHING.

DIANE VON FÜRSTENBERG

Life begins at the end
of your comfort zone.

NEALE DONALD WALSCH

LIFE IS NOT A REHEARSAL. ENJOY THE F*CKIN' LIMELIGHT!

There are exactly as many special occasions in life as we choose to celebrate.

Robert Brault

I HAVE FOUND THAT IF YOU LOVE LIFE, LIFE WILL LOVE YOU BACK.

Arthur Rubinstein

DON'T
WORRY ABOUT
TOMORROW –
BLOODY WELL
ENJOY TODAY!

IF YOU'RE ALREADY WALKING ON THIN ICE, YOU MIGHT AS WELL DANCE.

PROVERB

The most effective way
to do it, is to do it.

Amelia Earhart

GO GET 'EM
TIGER!

You can have anything you want if you will give up the belief that you can't have it.

ROBERT ANTHONY

When it is darkest,
men see the stars.

RALPH WALDO EMERSON

DON'T
LET THE
B*STARDS
BRING YOU
DOWN!

YOU CAN'T
EXPECT TO HIT
THE JACKPOT IF
YOU DON'T PUT A
FEW NICKELS IN
THE MACHINE.

Flip Wilson

SHOOT FOR THE MOON. EVEN IF YOU MISS, <u>YOU'LL LAND AMONG THE STARS.</u>

LES BROWN

WHEN LIFE GIVES YOU LEMONS, SQUEEZE 'EM AND ADD VODKA!

Life isn't about waiting
for the storm to pass;
it's about learning to
dance in the rain.

Anonymous

Change your life today.
Don't gamble on the future,
act now, without delay.

SIMONE DE **BEAUVOIR**

KNOCK
THEIR
F*CKING
SOCKS
OFF

HAPPINESS IS A WAY OF TRAVEL, NOT A DESTINATION.

Roy M. Goodman

Don't get your knickers
in a knot. Nothing
is solved and it just
makes you walk funny.

Kathryn Carpenter

RUN
WITH THE
F*CKING
BULLS!

Our greatest glory
is not in never falling,
but in rising every
time we fall.

OLIVER GOLDSMITH

DIFFICULTIES STRENGTHEN THE MIND, <u>AS LABOUR</u> DOES THE <u>BODY</u>.

SENECA THE YOUNGER

NEVER F*CKING STOP BEING A F*CKING BADASS

FIRST SAY TO
YOURSELF WHAT
YOU WOULD BE;
AND THEN DO
WHAT YOU
HAVE TO DO.

Epictetus

Opportunity is missed
by most people because
it is dressed in overalls
and looks like work.

THOMAS EDISON

BRING IT
THE F*CK ON!

LUCK IS A DIVIDEND OF SWEAT. THE MORE YOU SWEAT, THE LUCKIER YOU GET.

Ray Kroc

DON'T LOAF
AND INVITE
INSPIRATION;
LIGHT OUT AFTER
IT WITH A CLUB.

Jack London

DON'T BE A-F*CKING-FRAID OF GREATNESS!

WHEN YOU COME TO A ROADBLOCK, TAKE A DETOUR.

MARY KAY ASH

The season of failure is
the best time for sowing
the seeds of success.

PARAMAHANSA YOGANANDA

MAKE THIS THE BEST F*CKING DAY EVER!

It's never too late
– never too late to
start over, never too
late to be happy.

Jane Fonda

IF THE WIND WILL NOT SERVE, TAKE TO THE OARS.

Latin proverb

DOORS ARE MADE TO BE OPENED, BUT WALLS ARE MADE TO BE PUSHED THROUGH!

YOU CAN'T USE
UP CREATIVITY.
THE MORE YOU
USE, <u>THE MORE</u>
<u>YOU</u> HAVE.

MAYA ANGELOU

It is never too late
to be what you
might have been.

Anonymous

MEET NEW PEOPLE. NOT ALL OF THEM SUCK!

Always be a first-rate
version of yourself, instead
of a second-rate version
of somebody else.

JUDY GARLAND

Whoever is happy will
make others happy too.

ANNE FRANK

WHEREVER YOU GO, LEAVE A F*CKING IMPRESSION!

A MIND IS LIKE
A PARACHUTE.
IT DOESN'T WORK
IF IT IS NOT OPEN.

Frank Zappa

WITH THE PAST, I HAVE NOTHING TO DO; NOR WITH THE FUTURE. I LIVE NOW.

RALPH WALDO EMERSON

CARPE THAT F*CKING DIEM!

Have you enjoyed this book?
If so, find us on Facebook at
Summersdale Publishers, on
Twitter/X at **@Summersdale** and
on Instagram, TikTok and Bluesky
at **@summersdalebooks** and get in
touch. We'd love to hear from you!

www.summersdale.com